Family Violence

Ronda Armitage

RSVP

RAINTREE
STECK-VAUGHN
PUBLISHERS
A Steck-Vaughn Company

Austin, Texas

www.steck-vaughn.com

Published by Raintree Steck-Vaughn Publishers, an imprint of Steck-Vaughn Company

Library of Congress Cataloging-in-Publication Data
Armitage, Ronda.
Family violence / Ronda Armitage.
    p.   cm.—(Talking points)
    Includes bibliographical references and index.
    Summary: Defines family violence, explains its many forms, relates ways in which family violence can affect people's lives, and lists organizations that help people escape from violent situations.
    ISBN 0-7398-1371-4
    1. Family violence—Juvenile literature.
    [1. Family violence.]
    I. Title.
    HV6626.A745 1999
    362.82'92—dc21   99-26786

Printed in Italy. Bound in the United States.
1 2 3 4 5 6 7 8 9 0 04 03 02 01 00
33421001008829   10/01
DIRECT   18.95

Picture acknowledgments
John Birdsall Photography 12, 25, 31, 32, 36, 38, 41, 47, 48, 55, 56; Howard Davies Photography 53 (left); Format Photographers 6 (Brenda Price), 11 (Judy Harrison), 17 (Ulrike Preuss), 19 (Jacky Chapman), 49 (Raissa Page); Richard and Sally Greenhill 46; David Hoffman Photography 8, 20, 21, 24, 28, 43, 49; Impact Photos Ltd 26 (Steve Parry), 27 (Donna Ferrato); Retna Pictures Ltd cover, 7 (Philip Reeson), 15 (P. Reeson), 17 (Ewing Reeson), 22 (P. Reeson), 23 (P. Reeson), 39 (Jenny Acheson), 44, 54 (Jenny Acheson); Tony Stone Pictures (Getty Images): 4 (Bob Thomas), 5 (Stuart Cohen), 9 (Penny Gentieu), 13 (Zigy Kaluzny), 18 (Bob Torrez), 35 (Camille Tokerud), 37 (Peter Cade), 40 (Peggy Fox), 42 (Jon Riley), 50 (Howard Grey), 51 (Jon Bradley), 52 (John Beatty), 53 (right) (Thomas Renaut), 57 (Penny Tweedie), 58 (Christopher Bissell), 59 (Lori Adamski peek).

Contents

Discovering family violence   4

Violence toward children   12

Violence against women   24

Other family violence   32

The effects of violence on families   40

Stopping the violence   48

The future   56

Glossary   60

Books to read   62

Useful addresses   63

Index   64

Discovering family violence

Most people, throughout the world, live part of their lives in a family. It may be an extended family, with grandparents, aunts, uncles, and cousins as well as parents and their children. But for most of us it is the "nuclear" family, consisting of one or two parents, or stepparents, and their children, living in a family home. A shared set of values, religion, class, or caste are the important features. But the hope is that the couple will be happy with one another and raise their children in a loving environment.

However, evidence suggests that people are more likely to be killed, physically assaulted, or emotionally or sexually abused by other family members than by anyone else. Family violence, or private violence, is common not only in the United States and Great Britain but throughout Western Europe and many other countries around the world.

A happy wedding does not ensure a trouble-free marriage. Around a quarter of women in Western Europe experience domestic violence.

The place where people should be loved and feel safe is, for some adults and children, the most dangerous place of all.

Changing attitudes

Is this epidemic of family violence a new phenomenon? Are the stresses and strains of modern society too much for families to bear? In fact, families have been violent through the centuries, all over the globe. What has changed in the last 30 years is the concern about the damage to people and society caused by family violence. Family violence, once regarded as a private matter, is now recognized as a criminal offense. It is more of an open subject than ever before. Research shows that although women and young children are the two groups who are most likely to be the victims of violence and abuse, it can happen to any member of a family almost anywhere in the world.

Then why did it take so long to discover family violence? Perhaps because people did not want to know. They wanted to believe that the family was a loving place for all its members. Doctors treating the battered children could not believe that parents who should love their children could hurt them so badly. Men and women who had married for love were often ashamed and denied that violence was happening between them.

> ### Facts and figures
> The largest category of recorded assaults is domestic violence, and 80 percent of these assaults were against women.
>
> British Crime Survey, 1992

Although happy groups occur in countries throughout the world, violence may be just below the surface.

Myths and misconceptions

There are many myths about family violence. It may be that these have hindered people from finding out about, and understanding, the problem.

Family violence occurs only when people are mentally disturbed or sick.

This idea allows people to believe that violence doesn't happen in ordinary, normal families. It implies that only people who are sick could hurt someone they love. In a report in 1980, the sociologist Murray Strauss claimed that fewer than one-tenth of all instances of family violence were caused by mental illness or psychiatric disorders.

Family violence happens only in low income, disadvantaged families.

There is some truth in this. Researchers do find more reports of violence and abuse in poorer families. Lack of money, unemployment, poor living conditions, and limited education all contribute to the possibility of violence. But it is wrong to suggest that only families with these circumstances harm each other. It is possible that violence is more likely to be noticed in these families because there may be more regular contact with health and social workers. Offenders and victims of family violence come from every type of family. They belong to all social, racial, economic, and age groups.

Unemployment, poor housing, lack of money, and few prospects for the future can make for a very stressful family life.

Alcohol and drug abuse are the real causes of violence in the home.

Half the instances of physical violence in families in the Western world do involve alcohol. But half the assaults on women and children are committed by sober men. There are also connections between some illegal drugs and family violence. Amphetamines make people more excitable and lead to unpredictable behavior. An aggressive person is likely to become more aggressive and perhaps violent after taking certain drugs.

There is a cycle of violence: we cannot stop it.

Again this is a myth with some truth in it. Abusive adults are more likely to have been treated harshly as children than adults who are not abusive. The danger in this belief is that it scares people who have experienced violence as children into thinking that they are programmed to be violent and that perhaps they should not marry or have children themselves. But people can change their behavior and break away from family behavioral problems. It is important to remember that there are many people who were abused as children who do not grow up to become abusive adults. There are also some who have grown up in apparently peaceful families who become violent and abusive.

Battered wives like being hurt;
otherwise they would leave.

There are a number of reasons why many women do not leave violent relationships. Those who have grown up in violent and abusive homes may accept that this is the way things are. According to a report from Scottish Women's Aid, in their experience of helping over 10,000 women, they have never once encountered a woman who liked being battered.

Some people blame violence on alcohol. They excuse their behavior by suggesting "It wasn't really me, it was the drink."

Case study

The story of Kitty Genovese shows how reluctant people are to get involved in family disputes, no matter how violent. In 1964 a young woman, Kitty Genovese, was murdered by a man on her way home to her apartment in New York. Although many neighbors heard her screams and watched the assault from their windows, no one called the police. The young woman's death led many people to conclude that American society was corrupt and apathetic, blind to violence after years of watching television. On closer inspection this proved not to be the case. Many of the witnesses thought they were seeing a man beating his wife and therefore it was a "family matter."

Domestic violence is a criminal offense in the West. Yet many people regard it as less serious than other violent crimes.

Children's Charter

In many countries across the world, children do not have the chance or the power to speak out against corporal punishment. But in 1992, South African children's rights were set out.

"All children have the right to freedom from corporal punishment at school, from the police, and in prisons and at home ..."

Children's Charter of South Africa, adopted by a representative of children at the Children's Summit, Cape Town, June 1, 1992

In the United Kingdom parents can use "reasonable" chastisement when disciplining their children.

A definition of family violence

One of the problems in the field of family or private violence has been to develop a clear definition of violence and abuse. Richard J. Gelles, in his book *Intimate Violence in Families*, talks about two categories of violence: "normal" violence and "abusive" violence. "Normal" violence, he says, is the everyday slaps, pushes, shoves, and smackings that are considered an acceptable part of raising children or living with a husband or wife. "Abusive" violence is seen as being more dangerous, anything that is extremely likely to harm the person at whom it is directed. But there are some people who would regard some or all of these acts of "normal" violence as "abusive" violence and therefore unacceptable.

Also, what one culture may define as abusive may be legal in another. In Sweden, physical punishment of children has been illegal since 1979. Yet, in April 1990, Iraq passed an official order allowing men to kill their womenfolk for adultery, even if it was unproven. Defining family violence is difficult. Today, it is now a major concern in many countries. But severe instances that result in injury are still unusual.

Attitudes about punishing children

Using physical punishment on children is often regarded as unacceptable, yet in the United Kingdom in 1995, a large government-sponsored survey found that almost one out of six children had experienced "severe" physical punishment. The large majority—77 percent—had been struck in the previous year. More than a third of four-year-olds were struck more than once a week; three-fourths of one-year-old babies had been struck in the year before the interviews. A survey in 1992, in Romania, found that 84 percent of a sample of parents regarded spanking as a normal method of child-rearing. Some 96 percent of parents did not regard it as humiliating for their children.

What makes a family violent?

One anthropologist, Jill Korbin, stated in 1981 that where children are valued by the culture they are born into, they are less likely to be badly treated. In 1979 the sociologists Dobash and Dobash found that the more equal the partnership between adult couples, the more they shared decisions about money, child care, housework, and work, the less likelihood there was of violence between them. So it seems that violence is not something that has to be a part of family life. When people value and respect those they live with, violence is less likely to happen.

Research suggests that spanking helps to make children more violent and antisocial as they grow up.

Unwanted children

"All over the world and throughout history, certain children, who are perceived as having some undesirable quality, are often at greater risk of abuse. These include illegitimate children, orphans, stepchildren, girls, or retarded or deformed children."

Jill Korbin, 1981

Every culture and family deals with the upbringing of children differently. Respect and love help to make a more peaceful family life.

Talking point

"We are not talking about beating them up, but a little slap doesn't do any harm."

The Archbishop of Canterbury, Dr. George Carey, on bringing up children, 1997

"I think it is wrong to smack children and it will not teach them right from wrong."

Beryl Bainbridge, novelist, 1997

Which statement do you most agree with?

Violence toward children

Today it is taken for granted in the Western world that children have the right to grow up and to achieve their full potential. But this has not always been the case. Historically children have been seen as the property of their families, which were usually headed and ruled by their fathers. The term "child abuse," as we understand it, did not exist.

It is impossible to know how often children were beaten, abandoned, or killed. It was not until the nineteenth century that Western society began to recognize that the cruelty that some children experienced within the family might be called abuse and require that outside people or authorities be involved.

In 1874, the first challenge to the rights of parents arose from, astonishingly, the Society for the Prevention of Cruelty to Animals. Mary Ellen, a child who had been brutally beaten by her foster parents, was successfully removed from her home on the basis that "a child, as a member of the animal kingdom ... was entitled to at least the same justice as a common cur [mongrel dog] on the street."

In Asia there are still millions of children who do not have basic rights, such as the right to food and shelter.

Children in history

"In ancient times, infants had no rights until the right to live was ritually bestowed on them by their father. If this right was withheld, infants were abandoned or left to die."

Children in a World of Violence: A History of Child Abuse, by Samuel Radbill, 1987

In England, the National Society for the Prevention of Cruelty to Children was established in 1889, just over 100 years ago. That year, a bill was passed through the British parliament to protect children from cruelty inflicted by their parents.

In the United States, it was the work of physician C. Henry Kempe that raised public and professional concern once more. In 1962 he published an article suggesting that many of the injuries that were being seen on children at his medical center were deliberately inflicted by their parents. Since then the subject has rarely been out of the public eye.

The term "child abuse" is now internationally recognized. But it has different meanings for individuals and groups from different cultures. Much of the information about neglect and abuse has been gathered in European countries and North America. These countries have different traditions, attitudes, and behaviors toward children from those that might be found in, say, China or India.

Some people would suggest that shouting aggressively at a child is better than physical punishment, but others would say both behaviors are damaging.

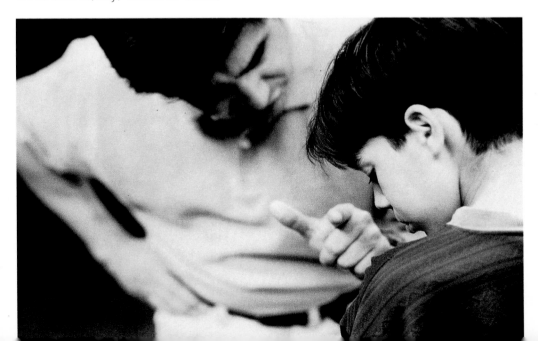

Much of the harm done to children is beyond the control of parents and care-givers. For example, in many of the world's poorest countries it could be said that the greatest threat to children comes from society. In Ethiopia children starve to death because of famine caused partly by civil wars. In India they work long hours in factories and sweatshops, for very little pay. And in Gambia, a baby's chances of surviving are low because of poor medical care at birth, common diseases, and dirty water. Many of these countries are worried about all forms of exploitation and abuse of children, but abuse is still a taboo subject and not openly discussed.

Most people would never consider causing deliberate harm and unhappiness to a child or young person. However, there are some families in which the rights and feelings of children are ignored and children are deliberately harmed in a variety of ways. Child abuse and neglect are generally divided into four main categories: neglect and physical, sexual, and emotional abuse. Sexual abuse is disapproved of in all cultures. But the definitions of physical, sexual, or emotional abuse differ from culture to culture.

In many Indian families there is an emphasis on corporal punishment. Its use is seen as an expression of parental concern rather than hostility to the child. The belief is that children must be trained to obey and that too much praise might make the child proud and difficult to control. In Europe and America, by contrast, corporal punishment is now actively discouraged, and praising a child is very much encouraged.

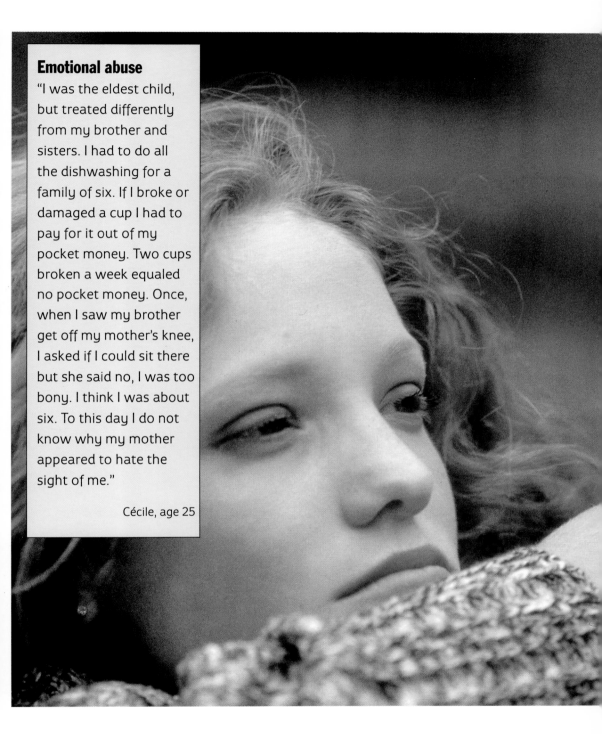

Emotional abuse

"I was the eldest child, but treated differently from my brother and sisters. I had to do all the dishwashing for a family of six. If I broke or damaged a cup I had to pay for it out of my pocket money. Two cups broken a week equaled no pocket money. Once, when I saw my brother get off my mother's knee, I asked if I could sit there but she said no, I was too bony. I think I was about six. To this day I do not know why my mother appeared to hate the sight of me."

Cécile, age 25

The emotional abuse of a child is sometimes difficult to detect.

In Great Britain there are four categories of maltreatment set out in the Department of Health's report, *Working Together*, in the Children's Act,1989.

Physical abuse

Physical abuse includes hitting, punching, kicking, biting, shaking violently, burning, and deliberate poisoning and suffocating. It also includes failure to prevent physical injury or suffering.

Neglect

Neglect occurs when basic needs are not met. This could include starvation, being kept in the cold or dark, or being left alone for long periods of time. It also includes failure to carry out important aspects of care that are essential for physical and emotional well-being, such as getting medical help when it is needed. Being thrown out of the house may also be an example of neglect.

Emotional abuse

Emotional abuse includes sarcasm, degrading punishments, ridicule, and withholding love and affection—anything that damages a young person's self-confidence and emotional well-being. Not getting one's own way all the time is not an example of emotional abuse.

Sexual abuse

Sexual abuse means forcing a young person to take part in any kind of sexual activity. This may include kissing or touching genitals or breasts. It may also include intercourse. Abuse might include asking a child to touch parts of his or her body or showing children pornographic magazines or videos.

Who are the abusers?

The abuser is usually someone who is well known to the child: a parent or stepparent, a relative, or a family friend or neighbor. In only six or seven of every one hundred reported cases of abuse of children is the abuser a stranger.

No one knows exactly why some adults take advantage of their authority over young people in this way. Research suggests that family stresses, caused by money worries, unemployment, and poor housing, are causes. When a parent cannot cope, he or she may take it out on the children.

The feeling of having no power in adult relationships or having been abused as a child may also play a part. Families who are isolated within the community, without extended family or friends to help in times of stress, may be at more risk of harm. One factor sometimes found in abusive parents is that they tend to have very high expectations of their children.

Some people have no way out of violent situations because they are poor.

Knowledge of child development allows parents to know what young children are capable of at each stage. This can lead to them "pushing" their children too hard.

17

Research suggests that mothers are more likely than fathers to abuse their children physically. However, in many societies mothers are still considered to be more responsible for their children's behavior and spend more time with them, particularly young children and babies. Although some women are sexual abusers, the majority are men.

Some adults say there is nothing wrong with the way they are behaving, that what they are doing is for the child's good. They will often try to persuade the child that it is the child's fault that the abuse is taking place. This is not the case; abuse is always wrong and it is never the fault of the child.

Raising children alone can place huge demands on a parent.

Some societies still do not admit that child abuse occurs. Russia experienced massive social, political, and economic upheaval during the 1990s. These conditions, combined with high rates of alcoholism and many single parents with little means of support, can be causes of child abuse. Yet until 1997 neither the general public nor the professionals in Russia acknowledged any child abuse problem.

In the People's Republic of China it was not until 1992, when three children were killed by their parents, that the country reluctantly accepted that there might be a problem, although the authorities insisted that there were only a "very few cases." Traditional Chinese culture emphasizes the principle of filial devotion, or *xiao*. The kind of behavior expected from a child includes, in extreme cases, sacrificing his or her own life for the parents' sake. Chinese parents emphasize parental authority and children's obedience through discipline that, in some cultures, would be considered harsh.

People line up for food in Russia, where social and political upheavals have resulted in cases of extreme poverty. This has often resulted in a breakdown of family life.

Case study

Deva, an Englishman, was 25 when he first went to counseling. This is his story. "I was eight when my uncle came to England from Canada for the first time. I can remember how excited my mother was. He was her only brother and she hadn't seen him for years. He brought lots of presents for everyone too, and somehow that made it all the more difficult. At first he just liked me to touch him and stroke him and then the abuse got worse. From the moment he started abusing me he seemed to hate me. He used to threaten me too, telling me how it would break my mother's heart if I told anyone. He said he was giving my parents money to help them out. Of course, that would stop and it would be all my fault.

He visited twice a year until I was about 13. Then I read something in a magazine and I realized that I wasn't the only one in the world this was happening to. So when my parents were out one day I called and told him that I never wanted to see him again and if he tried to do anything I'd call the police. I haven't seen him since. But I still think it must be my fault. And why didn't I stop it sooner, why didn't I tell someone? It all just goes around and around in my head."

Children are now more likely to be believed if they say they are being abused.

Reporting child abuse

Being abused by a trusted person can make it very difficult for children to tell anyone about the abuse. They may still love the person who is abusing them. They may not know that what they are experiencing is abuse. Because abusers, particularly sexual abusers, need to prevent anyone from finding out about their behavior, they will go to great lengths to ensure the person they are abusing remains silent. Sometimes children are bribed with gifts to keep the abuse a "special" secret. Or they may be threatened into believing that awful things will happen if they tell. They believe that the consequences of telling may be worse than the abuse itself.

Reporting child abuse is a big step, not only for the victims of abuse but also for the partners of the abusers.

What every young person can do

If you think you're being abused or have feelings or difficulties that may relate to having been abused when you were younger, please talk to an adult you trust, or call a hotline.

Talk to an adult

It is almost impossible for a young person to stop abuse, or recover from it, without involving an adult. If the adult you tell doesn't believe you, ask a friend to help you, but keep telling until someone does believe you.

Call a hotline

There are hotline numbers on page 63 of this book. You can call free any time of night or day. If they are busy, try again. Hotlines can help you decide whom to tell and how to tell them, and they can put you in touch with organizations that can help. You can call if you are being abused yourself or are worried about a friend.

Nowadays reports of child abuse are always taken seriously. In many countries there is a legal procedure laid down to protect the child. These procedures may vary from place to place, but most see the welfare of the child as being of major importance.

What happens when abuse is reported?

When a case of child abuse is reported, in most Western countries various professionals become involved. These may include a social worker and sometimes a police officer and a doctor. An investigation will take place in order to discover exactly what has happened.

A child considered to be in danger may be taken out of the home situation, but the majority of children stay in their own homes. After the investigation the family will meet and decide what help is required.

During this time children are encouraged to talk about their feelings and wishes and are kept informed about what is happening. If there is a high level of concern for a child's safety, his or her name may be put on a list of children who need protection.

When adults and organizations make decisions affecting children they should listen to what children have to say.

In the most serious cases children are required to give evidence in court. Although this may seem frightening, the professionals involved try to ensure that children suffer as little distress as possible.

Responsibilities, not rights

Societies have begun to accept that attitudes toward children need to change. This was recognized in the UK by the Children's Act of 1989. The new idea of parental responsibility shifts the emphasis from parents' rights over a child to their duties and responsibilities toward him or her.

The Act also insists that a "child's voice should be heard" and that their desires and wishes about their families should be taken into account.

Talking point

"Child abuse is the portion of harm to children that results from human action that is proscribed (forbidden), proximate (the action and the harm are linked), and preventable."

A definition of child abuse from two sociologists, Finkelhor and Korbin

What do you think child abuse is? Does this definition cover every aspect of abuse?

Love and anger

This quote from a Spanish child, Carmen, shows the mixed emotions often felt by victims of abuse.

"I don't know what to do. I'm 14 and my dad is making me have sex with him. Sometimes I feel angry and at other times I feel dirty and ashamed. I want to tell my mother but I'm afraid she won't believe me. I'm so confused because sometimes I love my dad, and I don't want him to go to prison. I just want the the abuse to stop."

Carmen, age 14

Children should be aware of their rights so that they can decide whether or not they are being abused.

Violence against women

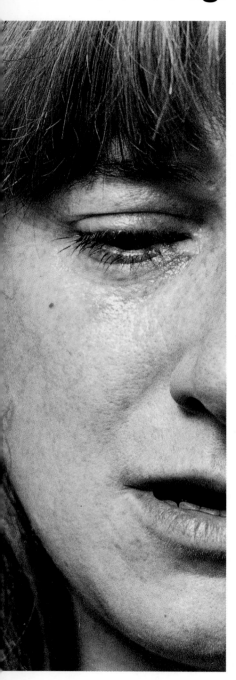

In 1981, the anthropologist David Levinson reported that the most common and frequent form of family violence was wife-beating. Until the nineteenth century, women in most societies were seen as being owned by their husbands and therefore of lower status than the husband. Physical punishment was often used to keep wives under control. A married woman's body, her property, her earnings, and her children all belonged to her husband to do with as he wished. Women were legally bound to stay with their husbands, no matter how they were treated.

The first changes

In 1848 the United States passed the Married Women's Property Act. Married women were granted a separate legal identity so they could work in their own names, although in most countries the right to vote was not granted until the twentieth century. In 1878 the English parliament passed the Matrimonial Causes Act. This allowed women whose husbands had seriously assaulted them to leave their husbands and get maintenance and custody of any children. Although great progress has been made in many Western countries, many developing countries still see wives as their husband's property and without any rights.

Changing mental attitudes

Legislation does not change mental attitudes overnight. Wife-battering continued behind closed doors. It was over 100 years before public attention was again focused on battered women. Women's groups began to organize "safe houses," or refuges throughout Europe, New Zealand, Australia, and the United States. By the 1990s research on wife abuse was being published.

Domestic violence can begin at any time in a relationship.

Marriage and violence

In 1993 Canada conducted the first national survey of violence against women. Of the 12,300 women interviewed, three out of every ten who were married or had been married reported at least one incident of physical or sexual violence at the hands of a marital partner.

Dowry-related violence

Other more unusual forms of violence are also reported. India has a problem of dowry-related violence. One case tells of a newly married woman whose husband and his family were dissatisfied with the dowry she had brought. She was covered in kerosene and burned alive. As in many other countries there is still no public record of the numbers of women who are violated, abused, and sometimes killed in India. This makes it terribly difficult to understand and deal with the problem.

Different attitudes

"You know, we Chinese have an old tradition of beating women. It still continues, particularly in the rural areas, but also in the cities, among all sorts of people. Women are beaten by their husbands and no one helps them."

Anonymous, Beijing, 1993

In some countries where women still have no power there are few agencies to listen to women's concerns.

In the last ten years there has been a significant change in the public response to violence against women in many countries in the Western world. This has meant that considerable progress has taken place in legislation to protect women. In 1994 the United States Congress passed the Violence Against Women Act. Three million dollars were set aside to reestablish a national hotline for victims and survivors of domestic violence. Money was given for more and better training for the police, to teach them the issues involved in family violence. The Act also included measures to increase the protection of battered women. Similar laws and services are now being put in place throughout Europe, New Zealand, and Australia.

But change has been slower in countries where the wife is considered to be a possession of her husband. A 1992 report from Brazil noted that wife-murder is a common crime, and that the men who murder their wives are often found "not guilty." It is seen as okay for a man to defend his "honor." Because women belong to men, any attempt they make to protect themselves is seen as a threat to their husbands. Many Brazilians believe that a husband is perfectly right to execute an unfaithful wife. It would be seen by the courts as an act of self-defense.

Female circumcision

Sometimes ancient traditions in a culture are abusive. Changing deeply held traditions such as these is a major task.

"I was circumcised when I was four. I hate it and I don't want it to happen to my daughter. I see no point to the painful mutilation that I have suffered and I feel that my family members abused my rights."

Kumba, age 21, Gambia

Some women will be beaten many times, over a number of years, before they ask for help.

Who are the men that batter?

It is rare for a violent act against a female partner to be a one-time occurrence. What starts as an occasional shove may in some cases turn into more regular violence. Abuse can be emotional, psychological, financial, or sexual, as well as physical. Now, in many Western countries, a man who rapes his wife is recognized as a criminal.

Men who abuse come from all walks of life, all classes, all ethnic backgrounds, and all ages. Most are violent only to their partners and not to anyone outside the family. Over half those men who are violent to their partners also abuse their children. Men who batter often have low self-esteem and very little sense of their own worth. Abusive men have also been described as feeling helpless, powerless, and inadequate. Violence is frequently used as a means of trying to display power over a partner.

When women share their experiences of a violent relationship they may be surprised by the sympathy and support they receive from other women.

The legal options

In most countries domestic violence is a criminal offense. The aggressor can be arrested and charged. On conviction, he may be sent to prison. Although some women may wish charges to be made against a violent partner, many, at least in the first instance, want only to protect themselves and their children from further violence. In many countries there are a range of orders or legal instructions that the courts can impose. These orders may exclude the violent man from the family home or the surrounding area. They can also order that he may not hit, molest, harass, or threaten either his partner or the children.

For some women, even with court orders in place, the risks of remaining in the family home are too great. Some 45,000 women a year in Great Britain flee to the safety of a refuge. These refuges also give support and practical advice. One of the aims of refuges is to give women the confidence to start a new life.

Often men who are violent have to be removed by force.

It's difficult to leave

Some women endure years of violence; others leave their partners for short periods of time but return again and again. The practical alternatives for a woman who wants to leave are still limited by many factors outside her control. She may have to give up her home, and leaving her partner or family can mean isolation and loneliness.

There are emotional considerations as well: wanting to protect the children, worries about being a social outcast, and feeling ashamed about what has happened. Many women feel very dependent on their partners; some women blame themselves for the violence and many even still love the man who abuses them.

Women who experience domestic violence often have very little confidence or self-esteem and feel totally powerless to change things. There is also the very real threat for some of retaliation by their partners.

The aim for the abused woman is for herself and her children to survive the abuse as safely as possible.

Women in Afghanistan

"In Afghanistan we cannot go to school and we can't go outside, even to the store, unless we are dressed in a tent and accompanied by a male member of the family. We must wear slippers, not high-heeled shoes, so that no one will hear us. The sound of our feet is considered offensive to the ears of men . . . We sit at home like birds in a cage. The Taliban [the group in power] say that women cannot work and girls cannot go to school, but there is nothing in the Koran that says this . . . . Other countries follow the laws of Islam but do not discriminate against their people in this way. Please hear our voices! Oh, God, why doesn't the sun shine on the dark world of women and girls?"

Anonymous girl, 1997

Talking point

"Anger causes violence."

"Sometimes there's no alternative to violence."

"Women are just as violent as men."

"Women want to be dominated by men."

"Somebody has to be in charge."

These are some common beliefs held by batterers. Do you agree with any of these statements?

Living in another country

Throughout the world it is common for people to emigrate from their country of origin. Some are granted citizenship in the new country, but for others this right is granted only when they marry. In the UK, immigration laws require that women who arrive in the UK may have to stay with their husbands for some time if they wish to remain in the country. This places an extra burden on women from Asian, Afro-Caribbean, and other ethnic minority communities if the women are involved in violent relationships. The cultural tradition of keeping the family together at all costs may already put enormous pressure on them to stay with a violent husband. And if the woman does leave, she could be deported, possibly without her children.

In some cultures the shame of divorce is so great that back home the woman may be cut off by her own family and the community and may even face violence from them. The concept of family honor has been violated. Some women in Jewish communities face the problem of having to keep up the myth that there is never any friction in Jewish families. This has again meant an enormous reluctance to report violence to the police.

Case study

Anita is 33 and has three daughters.

"In 1982 I came from India to be married. It was an arranged marriage but I loved my husband very much and after three years I had a little girl. Two years later I had another daughter and that's when my husband started to beat me. Girls are not valued in Asian society and I had produced two. I had to cope with his family telling me how useless I was because I couldn't produce a son.

"Then I became pregnant for the third time. I was so terrified that it would be a girl again that I cried all through the pregnancy. It was another girl so my husband was very angry. All the time shouting at me and beating me. Sometimes I felt so desperate that I just wanted to die.

"Then my husband took us to India. But one day he disappeared. We didn't have any passports, tickets, money, nothing. He went back to England without us. We were stuck in India for over a year. When I got back my husband told me he wanted a divorce because I couldn't give him a son. In my culture divorce brings great shame to a family; it is assumed that it is the woman's fault. Now I have nothing, no family and no money. He took everything."

Women are often ashamed to admit that they are in violent relationships.

Other family violence

Violence toward men, or husband abuse, has been a controversial area in the study of domestic violence. While there is no doubt that it happens, no one really knows to what extent. Some women suggest that much of it occurs when women try to defend themselves against abusive men, or, after persistent violence, retaliate and "give them a taste of their own medicine." Other cases show violence against men to be unprovoked and every bit as vicious as violence against women or children.

Violence within families is not confined to women and children. It can happen to other family members too.

The number of abused men is probably higher than previously thought, but the stigma of being a battered man prevents men from seeking help. When they do, there is little support for them.

Researchers have found a mixture of factors to suggest why women attack their male partners, including alcohol abuse and premenstrual tension, but in most cases there was no identifiable cause. The common feature was the woman's accusing her husband of being a "wimp."

Case study

Scott and Karen first met when they were at secondary school. Scott said, "I thought she was great. We started living together when we were about 19 years old and we got married when Karen was pregnant with Jade.

"That's when things started to get difficult. I really liked looking after Jade but Karen became very anxious. She didn't want me to touch Jade or look after her. She'd scream abuse at me for no reason. Then one day she told me that for years her uncle had sexually abused her and she was terrified that the same thing could happen to Jade. She didn't know whether she could be a good mother to Jade and protect her. And then the nightmares started. She'd wake up punching me.

"And then she started going berserk sometimes for no reason. Several times I couldn't go to work because I was covered with bruises. I couldn't tell any of my friends. They'd have suggested a good slap back to keep her in her place. But I couldn't do that. I knew how unhappy she was, she didn't mean to hurt me. I wanted her to get help but she said she couldn't talk about it.

"In the end Karen decided that she couldn't cope with Jade, that it would be better if I looked after her. So we live separately now. At last she's having counseling. She even jokes that maybe we'll get back together when she's got herself sorted out. I'm not sure I could trust her again."

Men who are victims of domestic violence may not know where to seek help.

Family fights

Younger children were more likely to have fights about possessions, especially toys. Young adolescents become very upset if a sibling invades their personal space. One father, driven to breaking point by his children's constantly fighting in the back seat of the car, took a can of red paint and painted boundary lines on the back seat and the floor.

From *The Cycle of Violence*, Steinmatz, 1977

Talking point

"Recent statistics from the United States reveal that 10 percent of all family murders are sibling murders."

Dawsan and Langan, sociologists, 1994

Some people believe that children's fights are a natural way to resolve conflict. Others think that this behavior is learned from parents who use physical punishment to resolve conflict.

What do you think?

Sibling violence

Sibling violence is so common that few people even consider it violence. Much of it is what has been described as "normal" violence: pushing, shoving, slapping, and throwing things. Most parents see it as an inevitable part of growing up and do not regard it as serious. They certainly do not regard it as criminal behavior.

In 1980, a team of sociologists conducted a survey on family violence that included sibling violence. On the evidence they collected they estimated that over 19 million children in the United States engaged in abusive violence against a sibling. This included kicking, biting, hitting with an object, and beating them up.

Children of all ages and both sexes engage in violence and abuse against brothers and sisters.

At all ages, girls were less violent than boys, but the difference in numbers was quite small. Teenage conflicts, although fewer in number, still took place. They were more likely to be verbally aggressive and to shout and yell at each other.

Sibling sexual abuse or incest is also not uncommon. Some of the sexual activity that takes place between brothers and sisters is sexual exploration, or what might be described as "sex play." The difference between that and sexual abuse depends on how much the child was physically or mentally forced into what was happening. Somewhere between two and four percent of children experience abusive sexual relationships with a sibling.

Children raised in nonviolent environments can learn to resolve difficulties with brothers and sisters in nonviolent ways.

Parent abuse

Many people find it difficult to believe that children might attack their parents. Parents have the position of power and authority in the family, and it is assumed by society that they decide how that power is used.

Violence from adults to children is still seen as a means of ensuring proper behavior. Children are smacked "for their own good." Society shows far greater disapproval of children who are violent toward their parents than the other way around, yet parents will often be blamed for their children's violent behavior. Because it is regarded as so abnormal, it is extremely difficult for parents to admit that they are being victimized by their children. They feel ashamed at raising such children.

Older children and young adults can and do inflict injuries on their parents in considerable numbers. In the United States, it is reported that about 10 percent of parents with a young person between 10 and 17 years of age living at home experience at least one act of violence a year. Three percent of these adolescents were reported to have kicked, punched, bitten, beaten up, or used a knife or a gun against a parent. In extreme cases, children have murdered their parents.

Some parents are afraid of their own children.

Who are the children who are violent?

Most children who behave violently are between the ages of 13 and 24. They are more likely to be sons than daughters. Sons' rates of severe violence appear to increase with age, whereas for daughters they decline as they get older, perhaps because aggressive behavior is still more acceptable in boys than in girls. Mothers are more likely to be hit and assaulted than fathers, although, as they get older, sons become more likely to hit their fathers.

The more violence children experience or witness in their home, the more likely they are to strike a parent. In instances when children, especially adolescents, kill a parent (parricide), they are likely to have been severely abused. In a few cases of parricide the child is severely mentally ill.

Although families are often happy units, living so close together can cause conflicts.

Family murders
In 1994, in the United States two percent of all family murder victims were parents killed by their children.

37

Abuse of the elderly

More people than ever before can expect to live to a "ripe old age." Better food, better healthcare, and improved living conditions have all contributed to an increase in the elderly population. This may account both for the increase in abuse of the elderly and the amount of professional and public concern. Although many elderly people may remain in their own homes until they die, others need to be cared for. Some will move into institutions, rest homes, or nursing homes, but many will move in with an adult child and his or her family.

Although all members of the household will do their best to adjust, difficulties often arise. Grandchildren may resent the interference with their lives. Sons and daughters who were looking forward to some freedom after raising children may also resent this new responsibility. The elderly person may require some nursing care, which can place a strain on the family's finances.

Some elderly people feel unwanted and lonely once they are no longer able to work and contribute to society.

Abusive treatment toward the elderly can take many forms. One elderly man was tied to a bed while his caregiver went out shopping. Some elderly people are physically attacked—injuries can easily be shrugged off as just an accident. They may not be properly fed. They may be bullied into changing a will or signing house deeds over to the caregiver. The elderly are often isolated, sometimes confined to their homes with nobody to tell.

Why are the elderly so reluctant to report their own abuse and neglect?

As with other forms of family violence, the victims often blame themselves. An important point too, is that the alternatives available to elderly family members, such as going into a rest home or nursing home, are often considered worse than the abusive situation they are in. So they keep quiet. Spouses of the elderly person are the most frequent abusers and there is an equal number of men and women who are victims.

It seems that violence can occur in any relationship where there is an imbalance of power.

Violence in gay and lesbian relationships

Perhaps the most overlooked form of intimate violence is violence in gay and lesbian relationships. In the 1970s and 1980s the use of the term "family violence" meant a focus on violence that occurred in traditional heterosexual relationships. There was also an emphasis on domestic violence as something men do to women. It did not include same-sex relationships. Prejudice about gay men and women kept many victims of gay and lesbian violence from speaking out about it.

What is now known suggests that the extent of the violence is at least as great as that in heterosexual couples. It includes physical violence, emotional violence, and sexual abuse. One particular aspect of emotional abuse may include "outing," or telling other people about a partner's homosexuality against his or her wishes.

The effects of violence on families

The consequences of child abuse can be devastating. Children are affected not only while they are being abused, but also in many cases for years afterward. In order to cope with abuse, children may develop a variety of strategies.

Victims of child abuse can become withdrawn. Because they feel worthless, they may seek to harm themselves or others.

Some will become very watchful—ready to avoid the blows that come their way; others may seem to invite the abuse, preferring that to the constant worry of wondering when it is going to happen. Some children become withdrawn and lose interest in themselves and their appearance.

Coping

"I had rituals to prevent the abuse from happening and of course I believed they worked. I did things three times (once for a wish, twice for a kiss, third time lucky) and I washed constantly, from my little toe upward, with cold water and carbolic soap. If I had a bad thought during this procedure, I had to start again from my little toe. This was terribly exhausting but completely necessary."

Anonymous victim of abuse, 1999

Feelings of worthlessness can lead some children to harm themselves. Or they may become very aggressive toward others and disruptive in school. Often this is because they are unable to deal with the overwhelming feelings of anger and confusion.

Children who have been sexually abused often feel "dirty," as if they have been doing something wrong. They may become obsessive about their bodies, constantly washing themselves. Some also show sexual behavior beyond their years and become sexually aggressive to other children. If they feel unable to tell about the abuse, children will try all sorts of ways to attract the attention of adults, hoping that they will notice that something is wrong.

Children often bottle up their feelings of fear.

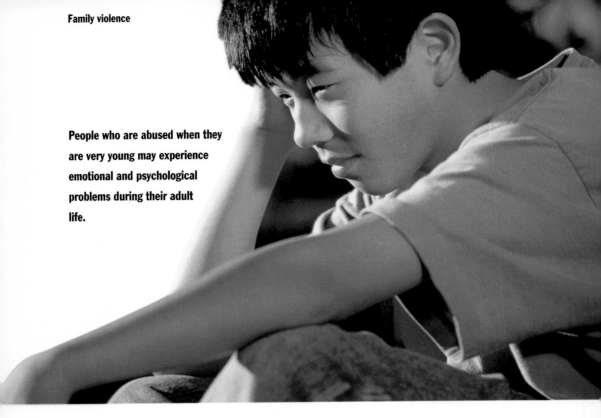

People who are abused when they are very young may experience emotional and psychological problems during their adult life.

Educational effects

In many homes where abuse is occurring, life can be very chaotic. Parents are unable to give children the time and attention they need. Some children may be unwilling to go to school, finding it too difficult to concentrate on schoolwork when they are there. As they fall behind in their studies they may begin to opt out altogether, failing to get the qualifications they need in order to get a job. Other young people throw themselves into schoolwork, relieved to have some distraction from the distress at home.

Long-term effects

Studies show that children who are abused may suffer disadvantages in their adult lives. They can find it hard to build lasting relationships. There is a higher chance that they will become involved in criminal activities and end up in prison. They also have an increased risk of alcohol and drug problems.

Costs to society

As well as the emotional costs to the maltreated child, there are also many consequences for families, communities, and society as a whole. The current cost of child abuse to agencies in Great Britain is $1.6 billion a year. Most of that is spent in dealing with the consequences of abuse rather than in its prevention. In 1994 it was estimated that in the United States it cost somewhere between $12,174 to $46,870 to care for each abused child per year.

Many people have experienced violence and abuse during their childhood.

Future problems

Young people who had seen a lot of violence between parents had problems at age 18. These included mental health problems, substance abuse, and criminal offending. Exposure to violence, started by the father, was associated with increased risks of anxiety, bad behavior, and crimes against property. Exposure to violence started by the mother was associated only with increased risks of later alcohol abuse.

Study from birth to 18 years of 1,265 New Zealand children, Christchurch School of Medicine, New Zealand

Surviving abuse

Although the effects of child abuse can be severe, many children who are abused and neglected do not show signs of disturbance either immediately after the abuse or in their adult lives. There are a variety of factors that may reduce the effects of maltreatment. These include having a good and loving relationship with an adult and doing well at school. Immediate help toward understanding the abuse can help too.

Effects of family violence

Studies show that, on average, women in Great Britain suffer an abusive relationship for seven years before asking for help. The stress of living under these conditions can bring other problems: lack of sleep, irritability, and nervousness and a range of other ailments such as headaches, backache, and depression. Some women become so despairing that they attempt suicide. Children may witness violent incidents or

With support and love, many abused children will show no signs of disturbance during their adult lives. overhear them. Mothers at a family center listed the effects that witnessing violence had on their children: fear, withdrawal, bed-wetting, violent behavior, and loss of trust.

Case study

This is Alison's story.

"I met Harry when I was still at art college. He was 10 years older than I; I thought he was wonderful. He was charming, intelligent, a successful businessman. Because I was so young I expected him to be able to teach me the ways of the world. Looking back I think it just gave him more power in the relationship.

At first it was little things. He'd criticize me in front of people and then laugh and explain that I was so young. And then it seemed to be happening all the time. I remember there was a time when he would hide things deliberately and then demand to know where I'd put them. Sometimes I thought I was going mad. Yet all the while I thought there must be a magic formula; if I find it everything will be all right. But of course I never did get it right, I was never good enough.

I think if things had continued like that I probably would never have left. The night that he hit me somehow jolted me. I hadn't experienced any physical violence before and I was quite clear that I would not let it happen. I knew about domestic violence. I didn't know that the other ways he treated me were abuse too. I left next day when he was at work."

Some women find it difficult to leave a violent partner and deprive their children of a father.

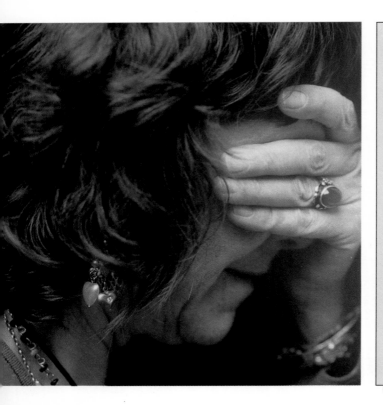

Everyone has a right to lead a life free from abuse. If the right is not respected it is the abuser's behavior that must change.

Leaving the abusive relationship

Many women do get out of abusive relationships. In 1993, 17,000 families in Great Britain were accepted for rehousing, where the reason given for leaving the last home was the breakdown of a relationship with a violent partner.

A change of home can really disrupt family life. Women have to take full-time care of children. There is usually less money available for essentials such as food, clothing, and household bills. Children may resent the lack of cash for toys and pocket money. Of course the relief from the fear of violence may override all these other difficulties, but it can be several years before families are sure that they are safe or before women gain enough confidence to take control of their lives again.

"Fifty percent of women referred to a mental health clinic were found to be victims of violence."

Hillman and Mason, 1978

Women often disregard their own needs and rights in favor of the other members of the family. Some feel it is their duty to keep the marriage a happy one, that they are more to blame when a relationship goes wrong. Do you think any of these ideas are correct?

The cost to society

It is almost impossible to estimate the financial costs of private violence in the Western world. There are negative effects in so many areas: medical and therapy bills for physical and emotional damage; prison costs for those convicted; housing costs after separation or divorce; working days lost by employers and employees; police and court costs. The list is very long. In London alone, according to official records, the estimated cost of providing advice, support, and assistance for those facing domestic violence is $455 million per year.

Wherever there is domestic violence, the professionals will also be concerned about all the components of that family.

Stopping the violence

In November 1989 the United Nations adopted the Convention on the Rights of the Child. This convention changes the obligations that we all have to children. One of the key statements of the charter covers the protection rights, which require that children be safeguarded against all forms of abuse, neglect, and exploitation. Many people now believe that corporal punishment, wherever it occurs against children, is a form of abuse and it does not work; even that it may turn into worse violence and is linked to the growth of violent attitudes and actions in childhood and later life.

Legal reforms banning all corporal punishment of children have been introduced in at least six European countries. Australia, New Zealand and South Africa are all giving them serious consideration. The purpose of these reforms is to change the attitudes toward violence against children.

Norway was the first country to have a spokesperson for children—a Children's Ombudsman.

Fighting back
A case in 1998, in the European Court of Human Rights, took another step in this process. The British courts refused to convict a stepfather for beating his stepson. The boy took his case against the British Government to the Court of Human Rights and won.

Women's rights

"Women in Brazil did not achieve the vote until 1932 and could not work outside the home without their husband's permission until 1962. Although the country's 1988 constitution granted full equality to women, the Civil Code still names the husband to be the head of the family and therefore the only one who is allowed to represent the family legally and administer the family finances."

Brazilian report, 1992

In the meantime, it often seems that cases of child abuse are just as frequent and horrendous as they always were. But throughout Western societies, public awareness has increased and with it a readiness to deal with this difficult issue. Those professionals who work with children and their families—social workers, teachers, doctors, and visiting nurses—are better trained to recognize signs of abuse. As a result, abuse is less likely to go on for years as it did in the past.

The state has the power to intervene in a relationship between a parent and his or her children if there are concerns about the children's welfare.

How best to intervene where cases of child abuse have been identified continues to be a dilemma for child protection agencies everywhere. There are those who suggest that more efforts should be made to control violence, that all those who are violent should be convicted and imprisoned for as long as possible. Others suggest that there should be more understanding of the abuser as well as his or her child victim. These days children are more likely to be believed when they tell of abuse, and wherever possible counseling and other services will be provided for them and their families.

Agencies need regularly to update their knowledge of all the resources available in the local area to victims of violence.

Whatever route is taken, it is accepted that the child's welfare is of prime importance. If it is impossible to prevent further harm to a child then the child must be removed immediately. Normally children do not want to be taken out of their families; they just want the abuse to stop and to feel safe.

In 1989, New Zealand pioneered a different method of working with families that is now being used in other countries. The emphasis is on keeping children and young people in their families and their communities. It is the family, not the child protection agencies, who are given the main responsibility for making the decisions about what will happen and how the child will be protected.

These decisions are made at a meeting of the young person and his or her family. If concerns remain about the safety of the child, then the preference is for the violent parent or caregiver to leave the home, not the child. This shows a willingness on the part of the state to look at a variety of ways to meet the needs of different families in different cultures.

Abusers may deny responsibility for the abuse. Counseling may help to change their behavior.

Rights for children

"Children should be aware of their daily rights so that they can decide whether they are being abused or not."

Childhood Matters,
Stationery Office, 1996

51

The rights of women

In most Western societies, certain rights for women are written into each country's laws. These include the right to food, shelter, and property; to decide whether or not they want to have children; to claim social security, get access to health care, and find employment. Other laws cover the right to political and religious freedom of expression, freedom from torture and slavery, access to education, and civil privileges such as the right to vote. In these nations women are given a right to a life free from all forms of violence. Such rights are not extended to women in some of the developing nations.

Different cultures give different rights to women. In many parts of the world, women's rights are only just being recognized.

In countries such as Bangladesh, where poverty is the main enemy, it is hard to help women who have violent partners.

In Afghanistan, the Islamic Taliban, the military and political force that controls most of the country, has prohibited women and girls from participating in many aspects of Afghan life. The Taliban justify all their actions by saying that they are following the words of the Koran, the holy book of Islam.

Sometimes the way women are viewed and expected to behave is shaped by religion or religious leaders.

Even in countries where women are protected by law, they often find themselves disadvantaged in everyday life. There is a preference in some countries for sons and the intentional neglect of daughters and females. These words from a Bangladeshi woman illustrate this point: "How can you explain to children that there is not enough food? When my son cries, I try to feed him. It is easier to make my daughter understand.... If there is less we eat less. You have to feed men more or they beat you. My son beats me if there is not enough food."

Whose body?
In China, the state prohibits women from having more than one child. In Brazil in 1990, seven-and-a-half million women of child- bearing age were ordered to be sterilized.

Case study

Brian, who is 30 years old, is currently serving a 7-year jail sentence for the rape of two women he met while working as a bartender. In prison he agreed to take part in an Offending Behavior Group. He then admitted that for years he had been physically abusing his wife Marie, and had raped her several times.

Brian has two sons. He has a history of heavy drinking. He would often go out "with the boys" on a Friday night

Modern women are less likely to view the man as head of the household.

to get "tanked up" and would return home in a bad mood. He said he then felt guilty for abandoning his family and drinking the badly needed family money; "It didn't take much to set me off." He now accepts that the violence cannot be explained by his drunkenness. "I wanted to do it; the booze allowed me to."

But Brian is still unable to accept that he was entirely to blame for the violence; he sees it as partly Marie's fault. "She should have kept away when I was in a mood, she knows what I'm like. She winds me up, she knows she does. Anyway a little slap never hurt anyone. I've certainly never punched her, that's a lie. And I certainly can't let her get one over me. I'm the boss in the household. I can't let my boys see their mother getting the better of me."

Failure to recognize equal rights for men and women gives men and women unequal power in society and consequently within families. Research has revealed that this imbalance is a major factor in family violence, particularly violence against women.

Changes in Sweden

Sweden, however, is regarded by many as a society in which there is almost equality between women and men. Yet despite several measures against violence in the last few years, thousands of Swedish women are still subjected to domestic violence. In 1998 the Swedish Bill for Action against Violence Against Women introduced a new offense, Gross Violation of Integrity, into the Penal Code. Its purpose is to deal with repeated punishable acts directed by men against women with whom they have a close relationship, but it also covers children and other closely related persons.

There is a continuing debate about what is most effective in reforming the behavior of men who batter. Some suggest that the law needs to change and that there should be tougher sentences for domestic violence. Others suggest that prisons are violent places and that unless work is undertaken to challenge men's behavior and effect some changes, these men may come out as violent as when they went in.

Kidnapped and beaten

In 1988, a young Algerian woman, born and raised in France, took refuge in a women's shelter after filing a case against her father and older brother who severely beat her, isolated her, and wanted to marry her to an unknown man in Algeria. However she was kidnapped from the shelter and taken to Algeria. She was drugged and beaten, her identity papers taken from her, and a marriage contract signed. She was rescued before her marriage by several women activists. The case was taken to the Algerian court and the woman won.

Equality between the adult couple and fair decision-making in the family provide the best opportunity for nonviolent family life.

The future

We need to get rid of all the accepted ideas that enable violent people to justify violence in society. Many people think that to ban hitting children as a child-rearing technique is a considerable step in that direction. But if that happened, many people believe we must also ban corporal punishment and capital punishment for adults. Some people say that the movies and television programs that glorify violence also encourage violent behavior and should be controlled.

Children must be protected from the terror of living in an abusive family.

Education

"One of the most important tasks we need to do, if we are to halt child abuse, is to educate people into understanding that humans cannot be owned by others and that physically producing and nurturing a child confers no more rights of authority than one holds over any human being. What it does, I think, is impose upon parents a duty to nurture in a manner that is respectful of children's rights to be treated as fellow humans."

Teacher from New Zealand, 1998

Research suggests that equality between the adult couple and democratic decision-making in the family provide the best opportunity for a nonviolent family life. But equality in families partly depends on laws that do not discriminate against one gender.

Case study

Ekwua was born in a village near Accra, in Ghana. After years of being abused by her husband she decided that she couldn't take any more. "Now I cannot understand why it took me so long to leave him. It is to do with our culture maybe. When I got married I was very proud of my husband and I thought that he was right about so many things. At first he would just slap me and I understood that I must have done something wrong. I thought that it happened to all women.

"I did not think then that I could leave him. I did not like it that the children could see these things. It was not good for them. Once when I went to the doctor I had bruises on my arms and she asked me about the bruises and she told me I didn't have to stay with him, she told me about the International Federation of Women Lawyers (IFWL). So I went to them and with their help I left with my children.

"Many of the stories we were told as children are about Ananse. He was always bold and daring while his wife was bowed down and uncomplaining. When things went wrong she always got a beating. Perhaps that was what taught us to believe that men were always right."

Attitudes toward women are shaped by traditional beliefs and ideas.

Bringing up children in the twenty-first century may be the most demanding job there is.

As disadvantaged families are more likely to experience family abuse, more needs to be done to reduce poverty and unemployment. Providing adequate housing, feeding, and healthcare could reduce stress in families. Reducing the social isolation of families within communities would be another significant step.

Provision of good-quality services such as day care, family centers, and home visiting programs—as a right for all families—whenever difficulties arise would be a positive move too. Society needs to think that families who call upon services have not failed, but that they have recognized that bringing up children and living in a family is a very hard job, and that at times most families will need help to do it well.

Talking point

"Children should be taught in schools, by a friendly teacher, that if anyone touches them sexually or beats them it is wrong."

Anonymous young woman, 1997

What changes would you like to see in the way parents, other adults, or people in authority treat you?

If more resources can be directed to support services for abused children now, then maybe the next generation will be prevented from being as abusive as this one.

In the last thirty years, great improvements have been made in many nations in response to family violence. If we can continue to work for an end to violence, then the twenty-first century could see an end to it. But we must push for change. There are still many countries where the family rights we take for granted are not yet even on the agenda.

Children have a right to life and the best possible chance to develop fully.

Glossary

Adultery Sexual intercourse between a married person and a person who is not his or her spouse.

Caste The different bands of social status that pass on through the family in Hinduism.

Chastisement Giving somebody a severe punishment.

Coercion The use of force to make someone do something.

Corporal punishment Physical punishment such as caning or beating.

Culture The customs and traditions of a particular people.

Deport To send someone away from a foreign country.

Dowry The money given to a bridegroom by his bride's family before the wedding.

Domestic violence Any incident of threatening behavior, violence, or abuse between adults who are married or who live together.

Explicit Very clear.

Exploitation Making use of something for one's own needs.

Female circumcision Removal of parts of the female genitalia.

Filial Relating to a son or daughter.

Heterosexual Meaning "different sexes." Taken to mean people who have sex with people of the opposite sex.

Homosexual Meaning "the same sex." Taken to mean people who have sex with people of the same sex.

Islam The religion followed by Muslims. Islam is widespread throughout the Middle East and India.

Legislation Laws.

Maltreatment Unjust or cruel treatment of a person.

Ombudsman An official who investigates people's complaints about the government or any of its branches.

Pornography The showing of sexual acts or explicit pictures with intent to cause sexual excitement.

Private violence Violence that occurs within a home or between people known to each other as opposed to public violence such as street violence, riots, or wars.

Prohibit To ban something.

Psychological Coming from or affecting the mind.

Sibling A brother or sister.

Society A social community, its way of life and organization, and its laws.

Sociologist Someone who studies society.

Spouse A wife or husband.

Stigma A mark or sign of disgrace.

Substance abuse Taking a substance such as illegal drugs or sniffing glue.

Violation The act of breaking a rule or failing to respect somebody's rights. The term is often used to describe physical abuse.

Books to read

Ackerman, Robert J. and Dee Graham. *Too Old to Cry*. New York: TAB Books, 1990.

Berger, Gilda. *Violence and the Family*. Danbury, CT: Franklin Watts, 1990.

Gilbert, Sara. *Get Help: Solving the Problems in Your Life*. New York: Morrow Junior Books, 1989.

Goldentyer, Debra. *Family Violence* (Teen Hotline). Austin, TX: Raintree Steck-Vaughn, 1995.

Haskins, James. *The Child Abuse Help Book*. Reading, MA: Addison-Wesley, 1982.

Hyde, Margaret O. *Know About Abuse*. Walker and Company, 1992.

Landau, Elaine. *Child Abuse: An American Epidemic*. Julian Messner, 1990.

Mufson, Susan and Rachel Kranz. *Straight Talk About Child Abuse*. New York: Dell, 1993.

Park, Angela. *Child Abuse*. New York: Aladdin, 1988.

Rench, Janice E. *Family Violence*. Minneapolis, MN: Lerner Publications, 1992.

Sources

A Sociological Perspective on the Causes of Family Violence by Murray Strauss in M.R Green (Ed.) *Violence and the Family* (Boulder CO, 1980)

Issues: Child Abuse Ed. Craig Conellan (Independence, 1998)

Child Abuse and Neglect: Cross-cultural Perspectives by J. Korbin (University of California Press, 1981)

Childhood Matters: Report of the National Commission of Inquiry into the Prevention of Child Abuse. Volumes 1 and 11 (Stationery Office, 1998)

Intimate Violence in Families by Richard J. Gelles (Sage Publications, 1997)

Murder in Families by J. M. Dawson and P. A. Langan (Bureau of Justice Statistics, Washington, 1994)

Ours by Rights: Women's Rights as Human Rights Ed. Joanna Kerr (Zed Books, 1993)

Useful addresses

American Association for the
  Protection of Children
63 Inverness Drive E.
Englewood, CO 80112
(303) 695-0811

Childhelp USA
P.O. Box 4175
Woodland Hills, CA 91370
(800) 422-4453

National Coalition Against
  Domestic Violence
P.O. Box 18749
Denver, CO 80218-0749
(303) 839-1852

National Committee for Prevention
  of Child Abuse
332 S. Michigan Ave., Suite 1600
Chicago, IL 60604
(800) 835-2671

National Council on Child Abuse
  and Family Violence
1155 Connecticut Ave., NW
Washington, DC 20036
(800) 222-2000

Immigrant & Visible Minority Women
  Against Abuse
P.O. Box 3188, Station "C"
Ottawa, ON K1Y 4J4
(613) 729-3145

White Ribbon Foundation
#104-220 Yonge St.
Toronto, ON M5B 8H7

Institue for the Prevention of
  Child Abuse (I.P.C.A.)
25 Spádina Rd.
Toronto, ON M5R 2S9
(416) 921-3151

Canadian Society for the Prevention
  of Cruelty to Children (SPCC)
336 First St., P.O. Box 700
Midland, ON L4R 4P4
(705) 526-5647

Kids Help Phone
#100-2 Bloor St. W.
P.O. Box 513
Toronto, ON M4W 3E2
(800) 668-6868

Index

Numbers in **bold** refer to illustrations.

abuse 4, 5, 6, 7, 9, 11, 12, 13, 14, 15, 18, 20, 21, 22, 23, 25, 26, 27, 33, 35, 37, 38, 39, 41, 42, 44, 45, 46, 48, 49, 51, 57
  child 12, 13, 14, 18, 19, 20, 21, 22, 23, 40, 42, 43, 44, 49, 50, 56, 59
  elderly 38, 39
  emotional 4, 14, 15, 16, 27, 39
  gay 39
  mental 14
  neglect 14, 16, 48, 53
  physical 14, 16, 18, 25, 27, 37, 39, 54, 58
  sexual 4, 14, 16, 18, 20, 21, 23, 25, 27, 33, 35, 39, 41, 42, 58
adultery 9, 60
alcohol 7, 19, 32, 42, 43, 54
arranged marriages **25**, 31, 55
assault 4, 5, 7
authority 57, 58

Bainbridge , Beryl 11
battery 25, 26, 30, 31, 32, 55
British Crime Survey 5

caregivers 38, 51
Carey, Dr. George. 11
castes 4
child abuse 12, 13, 14, 18, 19, 20, 21, 22, 23, 40, 42, 43, 44, 49, 50, 56
Children's Act 16, 23
Children's Charter 9
classes 4, 27
communities 17, 43, 51, 58
corporal punishment 9, **10**, 14, 48, 56 see also punishment
counseling 33, 50, **51**
crimes 5, 26, 28, 34, 42, 43
cultures 9, 10, 11, 13, 14, 19, 25, 26, 30, 31, 51, 52, 57, 60

deportation 30, 60
diseases 14
divorce 18, 30, 31, 47
domestic violence 4, 5, 8, 17, 26, 28, 29, 30, 32, 33, 39, 45, 47, 55, 60

drugs 7, 42

education 5, 6, 42, **48**, 56
emotional abuse 4, 14, 15, 16, 27, 39
equality 55, 56
exploitation 48

families 4, **11**, 14, 15, 16, 17, 29, **32**, 35, 36, **37**, 38, 39, 43, 46, 47, 50, 51, 55, 56, 58
family violence 4, 5, 6, 8, 9, 24, 25, 34, 35, 39, 37, 43, 44, 45, 55, 59
female circumcision 26, 60
freedom 9

healthcare 58
heterosexual relationships 39, 60
homosexual relationships 39, 60
hotlines 21, 63

incest see sexual abuse
Islam 53

Kempe, C. Henry 13

laws 24, 26, 52, 53, 55, 56, 57

maltreatment 16, 43, 44, 60
mental abuse 14 see also abuse
mental illness 5, 6, 37, 43, 47
murder 8, 26, 34, 36, 37
myths and misconceptions 6–7, 30

neglect 14, 16, 44, 48, 53
NSPCC 13, 21 see also societies
nursing homes and nurseries 38, 58

obedience 19
offenders 6, 46

physical abuse 14, 16, 25, 27, 37, 39, 54 see also abuse
physical violence 7, 25, 27, 45
poverty **6**, **12**, **17**, 53, 58
private violence 47
punishment 9, 10, 13, 14, 24, 48, 56

rape 27, 54
refuges 24, 28
religion 4, 29, 52, 53
rights 9, 12, 23, 24, 26, 30, 48, 51, 52, 55, 56, 59
Russia **19**

sexual abuse 4, 14, 16, 18, 20, 21, 23, 5, 27, 33, 35, 39, 41,
siblings 34, 35, 60
slavery 52
social workers 6, 22, 49
societies 13, 21
society 5, 6, 8, 14, 19, 23, 24, 29, 36, 38, 46, 47, 49, 52, 55, 56, 58, 60
  RSPCA 12
spouses 39, 60
stigma 32, 60
suicide 44
surveys and reports 6, 7, 10, 22, 25, 26

unemployment 6, 17, 58
United Nations 48

victims 6, 26, 33, 38, 39, 47, 49, 50
violence 4, 5, 6, ,7, 8, 9, 12, 17, 18, 19, 24, 25, 26, 27, 28, 29, 30, 32, **33**, 34, 35, 36, 37, 39, 40, 43, 44, 45, 46, 47, 50, 52, 54, 55, 56
  domestic 26, 28, 29, 30, 32, 33, 39, 45, 47, 55
  family 4, 5, 6, 8, 9, 24, 25, 26, 34, 37, 39, 43, 44, 45, 55, 59
  physical 7, 27, 45
  private 9, 47
  sibling 34, 35
Violence Against Women Act 26, 55

wife-battering 7, **8**, 24, 25, 26, , 27, 30, 31, 55

© Copyright 1999 Wayland (Publishers) Ltd.